For Roger

The quotes in this book are from Jane Goodall's autobiographies, *Africa in My Blood* and *My Life with the Chimpanzees*.

Copyright © 2011 by Jeanette Winter ▪ All rights reserved. Published in the United States by Schwartz & Wade Books, an imprint of Random House Children's Books, a division of Random House, Inc., New York. ▪ Schwartz & Wade Books and the colophon are trademarks of Random House, Inc. ▪ Visit us on the Web! www.randomhouse.com/kids ▪ Educators and librarians, for a variety of teaching tools, visit us at www.randomhouse.com/teachers ▪ *Library of Congress Cataloging-in-Publication Data:* Winter, Jeanette. The watcher : the story of Jane Goodall / Jeanette Winter.—1st ed. p. cm. ISBN 978-0-375-86774-3 (hardcover) —ISBN 978-0-375-96774-0 (lib. bdg.) 1. Goodall, Jane, 1934— —Biography—Juvenile literature. 2. Primatologists—England—Biography—Juvenile literature. 3. Women primatologists—England—Biography—Juvenile literature. 4. Chimpanzees—Tanzania—Gombe Stream National Park—Juvenile literature. I. Title. QL31.G58 W56 2011 590.92—dc22 2010005280 ▪ The text of this book is set in Aaux Pro. ▪ The illustrations were rendered in acrylic paint and pen. MANUFACTURED IN CHINA ▪ First Edition ▪ Random House Children's Books supports the First Amendment and celebrates the right to read.

20 19 18 17 16 15 14 13 12 11

THE WATCHER

◄ Jane Goodall's Life with the Chimps ►

Jeanette Winter

schwartz & wade books · new york

"Jane, Jane, where are you?"

"Jane, can you hear me?"

EVERYONE had been searching for hours and hours,

looking for little Valerie Jane Goodall.

Then, from the henhouse,

Jane came running to her mother, shouting—

"I know how an egg comes out!"

At five years old, Jane was already a watcher.

Jane watched ALL the animals in her world,

big and small—

earthworms, insects, birds, cats, dogs, and horses.

Jane quietly watched an English robin

at her window for days and weeks.

She saw him come close, closer,

then into her room to eat some crumbs off her bed.

When spring came, the robin even built a nest

in Jane's bookcase!

Perched high in her favorite beech tree,

Jane read about Dr. Dolittle talking to the animals,

and Tarzan living with the apes in Africa.

She wanted to go to Africa too,

and talk to the animals,

and live with the apes.

When Jane's school days were over,

she worked and saved

to buy a ticket to Kenya.

She hid her earnings under the parlor rug for safekeeping.

Crossing the ocean, Jane stayed on deck

and watched the waves, even when the cold wind blew.

She saw all the different blues and greens of the sea,

and fish that glowed through the dark water.

As Jane stepped onto dry land,

she closed her eyes in joy.

Jane looked for work with animals.

A famous scientist, Louis Leakey, was looking
for someone to watch and study chimpanzees,
to help us understand the animal most like us.
Would Jane be interested?
Yes, she would!

Jane traveled to the place in Tanzania where
the chimps lived—Gombe.

"I wanted to learn things that no one else knew,
uncover secrets . . . ," she wrote.

She set up camp, far from any human dwelling.

That first night, Jane lay awake listening to
new sounds—
the croak of a frog, the hum of crickets,
the laugh of a hyena, the hoot of an owl—
and looking up at the stars.
She knew she was Home.

At dawn Jane walked into the forest.

Up high she found a peak to watch from.

Every day she climbed to the Peak to look for chimps.

But though she could hear their pant-hoot calls to one another,
she didn't see them.

Jane walked down into the forest,
hoping a chimp would appear.

Still the cautious chimps stayed hidden.

Secretly they watched Jane.

When will I see a chimp? she wondered.

Then Jane fell ill with malaria.
Lying in her tent, burning with fever,
she almost lost hope.

But when the fever left her body,

she tried again

to get close to the chimps.

More weeks and months passed,

till one day the chimps let Jane see them.

She stayed in the background,

never hid,

acted uninterested,

and quietly watched.

Now Jane watched every day, all day—

even huddled in the rain.

She saw the chimps accept the rain,

not look for shelter, as we do.

And she kept notes about it all.

"You have to be patient if you want to learn

about animals," she wrote.

Some nights Jane even slept on the Peak,

to be near the tree where the chimps were sleeping.

She woke at dawn and saw them slowly rise

from their nests, sit for a spell, then go off to find food.

Jane named the chimps.

To her, each one was different—just like us.

A gray-bearded chimp was the first to approach Jane.

She named him David Greybeard.

"David Greybeard has—yes—

he has TAKEN BANANAS FROM MY HAND.

So gently. No snatching," she wrote.

David Greybeard let Jane come close.

She watched him shape a stick into a tool

to dig for termites.

Before this, nobody knew that wild animals made tools.

She watched David Greybeard eat meat.

Before this, everybody thought chimps ate only plants.

And because David Greybeard trusted Jane,
now the other chimps let Jane come close too.

"Chimps all around me. What a day—
chimps near, chimps far, old men, young men,
ladies, children, babies, teenagers—
the lot," she wrote.

Jane watched the chimps
when they were happy.

She saw them hold hands

and hug and kiss
and laugh—
just like us.

Jane watched the chimps
when they were angry or scared
and their hair stood on end.

She saw them swagger and throw tantrums,
and kept out of the way.

Jane watched the chimps at the Kakombe waterfall,
leaping and swinging in awe and wonder
at the tumbling water.

At night, after a supper of beans and tomatoes
and onions,
Jane listened to Mozart and Bach
as she wrote up her notes from the day.
Years of notes were piled high everywhere.
Jane needed help.
And so assistants came to watch and write.

One day Jane sadly left Gombe.

All across Africa, forests were being cut down,
and the chimps were losing their home.
Poachers were shooting grown chimps
and kidnapping their babies to sell to laboratories,
to the circus, and as pets.

Jane's beloved chimpanzees were in danger
of becoming extinct.
They needed Jane to speak for them.

Jane hated to leave her friends,

but she knew she must.

She traveled to big cities and small towns

the world over,

month after month, year after year,

asking for help to save the chimps and the forests.

Jane returned to the forests of Gombe
whenever she could.
She climbed up to the Peak,
calling "Hello!" to the streams and hills and trees,
David Greybeard at her side.

Jane watched, and listened again
to the pant-hoot calls of her friends.

And when she went back to civilization
to speak out for the chimps,
Jane carried with her the peace of the forest—

the forest in Gombe where
she talked to the animals like Dr. Dolittle,
and walked unafraid like Tarzan,
and watched and wrote,
and opened a window for us
to the world of the chimpanzees.

A Note About This Story

Jane Goodall grew up in England, but she dreamed of living in Africa. "I wanted to watch *wild* animals, not animals in cages," she wrote.

To simplify her story, I focused solely on Jane's own accomplishments. I omitted mention of her married life, her son, and her mother's unwavering support. Jane was twenty-six years old in 1960 when she arrived at the Gombe Stream Chimpanzee Reserve in western Tanzania to study the chimps. Because she was young, Jane's mother accompanied her to Gombe. But she returned to England soon after, knowing that her daughter could take care of herself. And so began Jane's life's work.

Jane referred to herself as the "white ape" that the chimps came to accept. Because of her patience, she was able to study the life cycle of the chimps, knowing some of them from birth to death. Her observations and writings uncovered many secrets of the animal world.

In 1986, Jane attended a conference organized around her groundbreaking book *The Chimpanzees of Gombe: Patterns of Behavior.* At the conference, she learned of the deforestation and destruction of the chimps' habitat all across Africa. And so she left her work and began speaking out to help save the chimps. She still travels most of the year, working to save animals and the land they live in.

Jane, the "white ape," wrote while in Africa,

"This is where I belong. This is what I came into this world to do."

And the animal kingdom is the richer for it.

I wish that when I was a little girl, I could have read about someone like Jane Goodall— a brave woman who wasn't afraid to do something that had never been done before. So now I've made this book for that little girl, who still speaks to me.

If you are interested in learning more about Jane Goodall, she has written a number of books about her life, including *My Life with the Chimpanzees* and *The Chimpanzees I Love: Saving Their World and Ours.* You can also visit janegoodall.org.